British Railway Picto

Cambrian
Lines

Rex Christiansen

Ian Allan
PUBLISHING

First published 2004

ISBN 0 7110 3006 5

© Ian Allan Publishing 2004

Published by Ian Allan Publishing

an imprint of Ian Allan Publishing Ltd, Hersham, Surrey KT12 4RG.
Printed by Ian Allan Printing Ltd, Hersham, Surrey KT12 4RG.

Code: 0408/B

INTRODUCTION

So much has gone, yet so much remains of what was once the largest of the Welsh railway companies. Since Nationalisation in 1948 the former Cambrian Railways territory has been reduced from almost 300 miles to 140. Surviving are most of the main line to Aberystwyth — switched from its English and eastern junction at Whitchurch to the far more imposing and convenient gateway at Shrewsbury — and the coastal arm from Machynlleth to Pwllheli.

The present shape of the system was the result of a British Rail plan to make the Cambrian lines 'the most up-to-date rural railway in Great Britain', as it was announced by the Public Affairs Department of BR Birmingham on the reopening of Barmouth Bridge in April 1986, which marked an important stage in the £4.7 million modernisation programme of the main and coast lines. But this was achieved only after years of cutbacks of the Cambrian lines and of the long single-track feeder routes from Bangor, Carmarthen and Ruabon. They had opened in a three-year period of Victorian railway expansion and closed within weeks of each other in winter 1964. All had been buffeted by Beeching. There was also the 2½-mile branch from Gobowen to Oswestry, providing a direct route from Birkenhead/Chester to Aberystwyth.

Ripping up the long feeders left the Cambrian as the only railway to Cardigan Bay. About 150 miles of track was lifted

Title page: It's the early summer of 1978 — 2 June, to be exact — and the tide is out in Barmouth Bay. As a small group of children wait patiently for the fish to bite, a four-car DMU formation heads south across Barmouth Bridge with the 12.14 service from Pwllheli to Dovey Junction. The train is formed of a two-car Derby-built unit at the rear with a refurbished Metro-Cammell unit leading. *Brian Morrison*

Above: No 7812 *Erlestoke Manor* climbs away from Fairbourne towards Friog Rocks in 1963. Barmouth is in the background (left), on the north side of the Mawddach Estuary. *Cooper's Railway Photographs*

CONTENTS

Introduction   2

1. The Main Line   5

2. The Coast Line   36

3. The Mid-Wales Railway   54

4. Branch-line Decline   60

5. Locomotives and Sheds   70

Chronology   80

on the three lines stretching through Wales from north to south. First to go was the 27-mile route from the Chester & Holyhead at Menai Bridge to Afon Wen; this was very much a seasonal passenger link, heavily used in summer by thousands going to Butlin's Pwllheli holiday camp, served by a station at Penychain, less than two miles west of Afon Wen.

More than 100 local authorities protested that the cutting of vital arteries between North and South Wales (and the tourist routes) was separating Wales, not unifying it. Written statements by objectors sent to the Transport Users' Consultative Committee (TUCC) for Wales & Monmouthshire ran to more than 60 pages. Contributors ranged from local authorities and the Chief Constable of Gwynedd, who felt that the local road system was not suitable for the heavy traffic in summer (in 1965 Butlin's had 111,000 visitors), to occasional travellers like a woman living in Manchester, who stated that she was a regular traveller to the area at least four times a year, arriving either at Chwilog or Afon Wen.

Bangor–Afon Wen closed as a through route on 7 December 1964. Transport Minister Ernest Marples had rejected proposals to close the whole of the branch, retaining Bangor–Caernarvon because it was a useful railhead for places further south, including Butlin's. The stub survived until February 1972.

Menai Bridge–Afon Wen had formerly been LNWR territory, but the second and third of the lines closed — the 56-mile former Manchester & Milford line between Aberystwyth and Carmarthen and the charming, scenic 53-mile route through the Dee Valley from Ruabon to Morfa Mawddach (formerly Barmouth Junction) — had been GWR, the eight miles west from Dolgelley to Barmouth Junction being formed of the original Cambrian branch, on which trains had used a joint station at Dolgelley. Llangollen (Goods Junction)–Dolgellau (as it was by now spelled) was closed officially on 18 January 1965, although floods had actually severed the line a few weeks earlier.

Although listed (with its offshoot from Bala to Blaenau Ffestiniog) for closure in the Beeching Report, Ruabon–Morfa Mawddach was considered for reprieve because of its secondary importance to the Cambrian as a through route to the coast from North West England. But as a secondary route it was closed in line with contemporary thinking that secondary lines could be dispensed with. The Vale of Rheidol survived closure proposals thanks to the efforts of George Dow when he was Divisional Manager at Stoke-on-Trent.

Shrewsbury–Aberystwyth was never under threat, because of the importance of several small but growing towns — Welshpool, Newtown and Machynlleth — it served *en route*. But the claims of Oswestry to retain a railway were ignored. Ruabon–Morfa Mawddach is remembered as part of the only GWR line in North Wales until the company acquired the Cambrian system at the Grouping.

One of the best-remembered innovations of the Nationalised years were the Land Cruise trains, which made round-trips in both directions between the North Wales and Mid-Wales coasts during the period 1951-61. They were immediately popular with holidaymakers, and the services were increased and days added to those on which they were originally scheduled. How many passengers subsequently took holidays at places they had seen through carriage windows or had visited when 'land cruising' will never be known, but it has been suggested that such trains encouraged tourists to explore places they had never thought to visit before.

One tradition that never changed for many years was the constant effort by railway companies to encourage holidaymakers and day trippers to the coast. Wales & Borders Trains, predecessor to Arriva (which took over with a 15-year franchise on 7 December 2003), did so with fervour verging on the poetic in its bilingual pocket timetables: 'The route is stunning, the scenery is breathtaking, the history is spectacular — come back again and again to see it all!'

Detailed histories of the lines can be found in more than 50 books on the subject of Welsh Railways, as well as in tourist guides and in timetables ancient and modern, passenger and freight. I owe special thanks to Bob Miller (co-author of two volumes of *The Cambrian Railways*), Harold Forster MBE (formerly Area Manager at Wrexham and later Manchester Piccadilly), Gordon Biddle and Peter Waller. I have also enjoyed help from fellow members of the Railway & Canal Historical Society and also, over many years, of the Wirral Railway Circle.

Rex Christiansen
Chelford
March 2004

Left: Oswestry was the home of the Cambrian Railways and, as might be expected, was provided with substantial offices and workshops. With the company's erstwhile offices in the background, BR Standard 4-6-0 No 75021 stands in the station with a service towards Whitchurch. *SLS collection*

Overleaf: Map of the erstwhile Cambrian Railways system at its greatest extent, prior to takeover by the GWR in 1922.

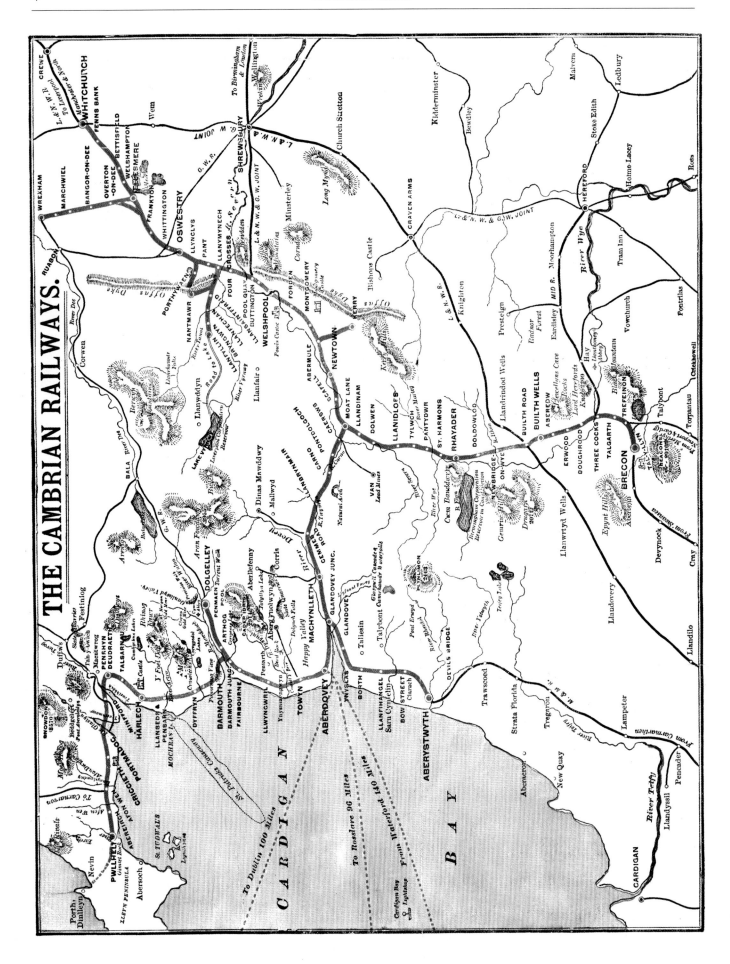

THE CAMBRIAN RAILWAYS.

1. THE MAIN LINE

Shrewsbury has been the only gateway to the Cambrian coast since the closure of the 31 miles of the original Cambrian main line between Whitchurch and Buttington on 18 January 1965. Trains were diverted thereafter over the former Shrewsbury & Welshpool GWR/LNWR Joint line, on which the six wayside stations had already been closed, in 1960, including Buttington, one of the largest and most isolated four-platformed stations in Britain, which had two platforms on both the Whitchurch and Shrewsbury lines.

The *Border Counties Advertizer* lamented that the Whitchurch–Welshpool closure was, apart from the trusty old 'Gobowen Flier', the end of the line for Oswestry too:

'For the railway employees this final blow means an uncertain wait and the threat of redundancy. Two men who represent the Loco Departmental Committee at Oswestry say that a statement last week that 22 men from Oswestry will be going to Shrewsbury to fill vacancies left by men retiring voluntarily, is incorrect. They say those vacancies will go to Shrewsbury men who are redundant and there will still be about 60 drivers and firemen at Oswestry with an uncertain future.'

Closure between Buttington and Whitchurch also severed the Cambrian's last link with the Shropshire & Montgomeryshire Railway at Llany-mynech and that from Ellesmere to Wrexham, the biggest town in North Wales. When final closure came at Oswestry, it was the Great Western (not the Cambrian) whose line achieved the distinction of being the first to reach the town and the last to leave.

The 2¼-mile branch from the Shrewsbury & Chester main line at Gobowen had opened in 1848 — 12 years ahead of the Cambrian main line from Oswestry to Pool Quay — and by 7 November 1966, when the 'Gobowen Flier' ended, it had outlived the Cambrian by over a year. Oswestry Carriage & Wagon shops had closed in the summer of 1964, and the Locomotive Works' repair section in January 1966, complete closure following in January 1967.

As it turned out, this was not quite the end of the railway scene at Oswestry, for a single line through the empty station was

kept open until 1988 for use by stone trains to the Nantmawr quarries. (In the 1960s this had been used for track-lifting trains on the Llanfyllin branch soon after closure.) Today, Oswestry station yard is the headquarters of the Cambrian Railways Society, which aims to open eight miles of mothballed track, initially between Gobowen and Oswestry and progressively south to Porthywaen and Blodwell.

A number of changes which took place under Western Region control of the Cambrian Lines were reflected in passenger and freight Working Timetables. In the winter of 1955 that for the WR's Oswestry District was issued by the Chief Operating Superintendent (Paddington). The area covered stretched from Wrexham and Whitchurch to Carmarthen, joining the Swansea District at Pencader, and over the Mid-Wales Railway via Talyllyn Junction to join the Newport District at Pontsticill.

By the summer of 1962 the Oswestry operating area had contracted; redesignated as Shrewsbury District (Oswestry Area), it no longer included Aberystwyth–Carmarthen, although the former Manchester & Milford route was still open. The Mid-Wales line in its final months ended at Three Cocks Junction, a short distance north of which was the boundary between Newport and Shrewsbury Districts. The Working Timetable was now issued by the District Traffic Manager (Cardiff).

Further administrative change came in January 1963, when the Cambrian Lines were transferred to the London Midland Region, initially controlled from Chester

Above: The years following Nationalisation saw a few minutes cut from the timings of some of the more important services between Aberystwyth, Shrewsbury and Crewe. In 1957 the mid-day departure from Aberystwyth reached Oswestry in about four hours and took a further 90 minutes to cover the 30 miles to Crewe. Collett 0-6-0 No 2239 was in charge of the Crewe portion when seen at Oswestry in 1957. Such trains never seemed as impressive or important as when they were hauled by 'Manor' 4-6-0s. *Ian Allan Library/ J. A. Peden*

and later by the Divisional Manager at (Stoke-on-Trent).

In the 1950s and 1960s there were many timetable and operating changes. In a fresh attempt to attract more passengers, the Western Region restored the name of the 'Cambrian Coast Express', running from Paddington via Birmingham to Aberystwyth and the coast. To try to get better connections with North West England and Yorkshire it began reversing at Shrewsbury instead of using the Abbey avoiding line. The 'CCE' would run in modified form until 1991 but will be remembered as a titled train which changed its character in mid-journey from a main-line express (between Paddington and Birmingham Snow Hill) to a local stopping service (beyond Welshpool).

In May 1964 the London Midland Region announced its intention to close 14 stations and halts between Shrewsbury and Aberystwyth. The total was reduced when the Transport Minister accepted that the closure of Caersws would cause some hardship to local people; the Minister had stipulated the introduction of a school bus between Newtown and Talerddig, but this was rescinded after he stated that the requirement had been planned in error. The station closures included Llandre and Glandyfi (which had survived a similar attempt in 1953), to allow the acceleration of the 3.15pm Shrewsbury–Aberystwyth service.

Rationalisation took place in June 1965 with the introduction of a weekday-only DMU service between Shrewsbury and Aberystwyth, which remains the most sweeping operational change since Nationalisation. Intermediate stops were reduced to Welshpool, Newtown, Caersws, Machynlleth, Dovey Junction and Borth. All increased in importance as railheads serving large, mostly rural areas. Average journey times of steam trains were cut by 35 minutes, to 2hr 35min.

Since Nationalisation Shrewsbury–Aberystwyth timings have been almost halved, to around two hours, but the speed-up on the coast line has been limited to about 20 minutes, because of operating difficulties and still closely packed stations and halts. The Winter 2003 timetable showed 15 halts as requests.

Freight services on the Cambrian ebbed away slowly over the years — at about the same pace at which they ran. In the winter of 1956 the 9.30am goods over the main line from Oswestry to Moat Lane Junction was not booked to leave Welshpool until 2½ hours later. The schedule included 35 minutes allowed for crossing an up train at Four Crosses. The timings were still the same some seven years later, by which time the service had been reduced to Mondays, Wednesdays and Fridays only.

A major modernisation was the introduction of radio signalling (RETB) in 1988 between Sutton Bridge Junction, Shrewsbury and Aberystwyth/Pwllheli. The scheme included a signalling centre in the 'box at Machynlleth.

Changes to the main line have included the replacement of Welshpool station in the summer of 1992, after the trackbed was used for the construction of a relief road to carry the main North–South Wales road (A483) clear of the town. The old station, a listed building, was restored to its Cambrian glory and converted into a shopping centre once a new, more modest station had been built on a new alignment to the east of the original.

In the winter of 1978 BR began extending and speeding-up the introduction of bilingual station signs, citing as examples Y Bermo/Barmouth. Such signs had begun appearing on the Cambrian years earlier, Barmouth Junction being shown as Morfa Mawddach as early as June 1960.

Right: Engine whistle codes introduced five years before Nationalisation continued in use until four years afterwards. Issued in the Service Timetable Appendix from Oswestry in March 1943, they were replaced by the first supplement to the Appendix issued on 27 April 1952. The latter stressed that, to avoid annoying passengers at stations and residents of neighbourhoods near the railway, drivers must not use whistles more than absolutely necessary. *Author's collection*

Upper left: The Cambrian main line of today took final shape when the Welshpool–Oswestry–Whitchurch through services were switched to Shrewsbury after the section closed on 18 January 1965, when an SLS special departed Oswestry for Whitchurch behind ex-GWR 4-6-0 No 7802 *Bradley Manor.* This was a day of slaughter on the railways of mid-Wales, no fewer than eight routes being closed to passengers, including most of the GWR secondary route between Ruabon and Morfa Mawddach. *R. W. Miller*

Lower left: Oswestry remained on the BR passenger map until November 1966, when Gobowen motor trains over the former GWR branch ceased. 0-4-2 tank No 1432 departs Oswestry in 1953, passing the former GWR station just to the north of the Cambrian station and head offices. The station became the town's goods depot after the GWR and Cambrian depots were amalgamated in 1924. In BR days Gobowen-branch freight services outlived those for passengers by five years. *Ian Allan Library*

Upper right: Oswestry was the hub of rural branches straddling the Welsh border and serving small towns. The longest was through the Tanat Valley to Llangynog, at the foot of the Berwyn Mountains, which rise to over 2,700ft. The ex-Cambrian 2-4-0 tank — GWR No 1197 — worked in the valley for many years, being seen at Oswestry on 13 March 1948. Three years later the Tanat branch was closed to passengers, although part survived for freight and mineral traffic from quarries for some time. *SLS collection*

Centre right: Whitchurch (LNWR), looking towards Crewe — the scene in June 1967, 2½ years after it ceased to be a junction for Oswestry (the LNWR Whitchurch–Tattenhall Junction branch having closed in December 1963). *Andrew Muckley*

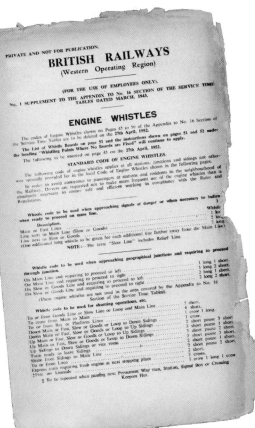

Right: On 28 July 1962 the first of the 'Manor' class, No 7800 *Torquay Manor*, enters Llanymynech station with the 9.45am service from Whitchurch to Aberystwyth. Built in January 1938 (Lot 316), No 7800 would survive in service until August 1964. Passenger services over the line from Oswestry to Buttington Junction would not last much longer, being withdrawn from 18 January 1965. *Leslie Sandler*

Above: Buttington was the junction for the ex-GW/LNWR line from Shrewsbury. On 25 July 1959 'Dukedog' No 9001 arrives in the station with a down service from Shropshire's county town. Buttington station was destined to close just over a year later, on 12 September 1960. *R. K. Blencowe*

Below: An unidentified up service, probably the 'Cambrian Coast Express', at Welshpool — its last stop on former Cambrian territory — during the summer of 1963, in the charge of BR Standard 4-6-0 No 75004. Welshpool was some 62 miles from Aberystwyth and 172 miles from Paddington. The journey time was then 6hr 10min. *Ian Allan Library*

Above:
The end of civilian rail traffic over the Shropshire & Montgomeryshire Railway in the winter of 1960 left Llanymynech as the only junction handling military traffic — and then for only a short while longer. *Author's collection*

Below: Forden was one of 13 main-line stations closed in June 1965. When BR put the station house on the market 10 years later it advertised one of its attractions as being 'easy motoring distance, Cambrian Coast'! *Author's collection*

MID-WALES
Easy motoring distance
Cambrian Coast
STATION HOUSE FORDEN,
Nr. Welshpool. 5 Rooms.
Ample ground space. Rural
area. Ref.: 88. By order of
British Rail Property Board,
Morris, Marshall & Poole,
Welshpool Tel: 2717.

Above: Again unidentified, an up service at Welshpool in the charge of No 7827 *Lydham Manor*. In the summer of 1963 the 'Cambrian Coast Express' was shown as including through coaches from Aberystwyth and Pwllheli to Paddington, with a restaurant car added at Shrewsbury. *Ian Allan Library*

Below: On 21 August 1963 'Manor' 4-6-0 No 7819 *Hinton Manor* arrives at Welshpool with the down 'Cambrian Coast Express'. *R. N. Joanes*

Right: A '2251' 0-6-0, No 3200, arrives at Welshpool on 28 July 1962 at the head of the 7.35am service from Aberystwyth to Shrewsbury. The locomotive will be replaced here by Fowler-designed 2-6-4T No 42385. Behind the ex-LMS locomotive is '43xx' 2-6-0 No 7302, which will provide the motive power for the 10.10am service to Shrewsbury. *Leslie Sandler*

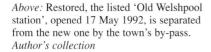

Above: Restored, the listed 'Old Welshpool station', opened 17 May 1992, is separated from the new one by the town's by-pass. *Author's collection*

Centre right: The changing scene at Abermule in the mid-1960s, as seen from an Aberystwyth–Shrewsbury service meeting a coast-bound DMU. *Andrew Muckley*

Lower right: Like Welshpool, Newtown was one of the principal stops on the main line, where trains often passed. In the autumn of 1963 No 7822 *Foxcote Manor* (now preserved) heads a coast-bound semi-fast. *Andrew Muckley*

Above: The busy goods yard at Newtown being shunted by an Ivatt '464xx' Mogul, as seen from the cosy cab of Standard 2-6-4 tank No 80131 on 29 January 1964. *Author's collection*

Below: A crew-training DMU passes Moat Lane West 'box in August 1964. Opened in 1859, as the Mid-Wales Railway was pressing south towards Brecon, the attractive little 'box, controlling the entrance to Moat Lane two-road engine shed, was rebuilt in the mid-1950s, having (it was said) almost fallen down with age. *Andrew Muckley*

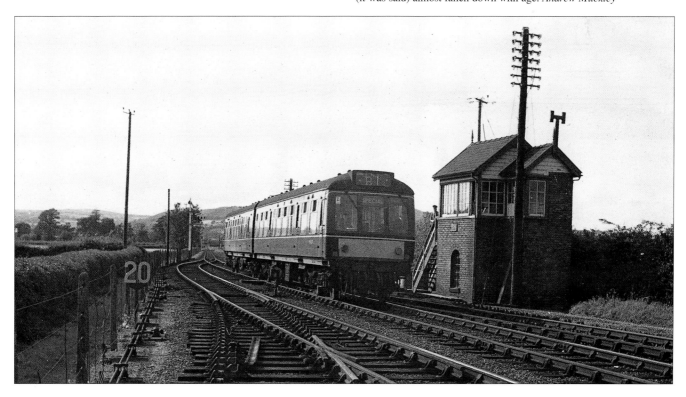

Upper left: Moat Lane station was part of an attractive isolated junction between the main line and the route to Brecon. The substantial station, with platforms serving both lines, included a large refreshment room, because passengers changing between them often faced long delays. *Andrew Muckley*

Lower left: Tablet exchange at Moat Lane West 'box between the signalman and the crew of a Shrewsbury-bound stopping train in 1965. Partially obscured by steam, the station is in the background (centre). *Andrew Muckley*

Upper right: Caersws station, on the main line, was one of two in the village (although the other had not been in passenger use since Victorian times). Originally the lower terminus of the Van Railway (1871-1940), which ran 6½ miles to lead mines in the hills, it had a down loop but lacked a platform. No 7827 *Lydham Manor* calls with an Aberystwyth stopping train in the summer of 1963. Caersws ex-Cambrian station is still open today. *Andrew Muckley*

Centre right: Long-distance main-line services were supplemented by shorter workings like the 4.20pm from Newtown to Machynlleth. In August 1964 Class 3 2-6-2 tank No 82005 approaches Caersws with the 54min working. *Andrew Muckley*

Below: The preceding train, at 2.40pm, was the 'Cambrian Coast Express', which made seven fewer stops, taking 50 minutes to Machynlleth. No 7819 *Hinton Manor* climbs towards Pont Dolgoch in August 1964. *Andrew Muckley*

Above: Towards the end of steam, Cambrian freights were made up of a large variety of ageing vehicles. No 7807 *Compton Manor* enters Carno down loop prior to passing the 'box in August 1964. *Andrew Muckley*

Below: Another study of a 'Manor' freight working — No 7821 *Ditcheat Manor* near Carno with a local working from Aberystwyth, also in August 1964. *Andrew Muckley*

Above: Ex-GWR '43xx' Mogul No 6368 calls at Carno, stopping beside a collection of luggage and porters' trolleys filling the sheltered waiting area on the up platform. *Andrew Muckley*

Below: Carno closed at the start of the 1965 summer timetable. In September 1966 a coast-bound stopping train headed by Standard 4-6-0 No 75002 passes the station site and its 'box, from which the nameplate has been removed. *Andrew Muckley*

Above: No 7822 *Foxcote Manor* lets off steam on departure from Carno with a coast-bound service made up of a mixture of corridor stock. *Andrew Muckley*

Below: A Standard Class 2 Mogul leaves Carno with a morning Machynlleth–Newtown local service in the autumn of 1963. Having departed Machynlleth at 7.35am, this train would take a total of 65 minutes to reach its destination. *Andrew Muckley*

Top: On 6 August 1966 BR 'Standard 4' 4-6-0 No 75002 approaches Talerddig station with a service from London to Aberystwyth.
Derek Cross

Centre: Engines of freight trains climbing to the main-line summit at Talerddig (693ft) had to stop at the up starting signal for banking engines to be detached. The movement was controlled by the signalman in Talerddig 'box, among the most isolated on the line.
Ian Allan Library

Right: Having climbed Talerddig Bank, '2251' 0-6-0 No 2219 passes through Talerddig station with a freight from Machynlleth to Oswestry on 10 July 1957.
Stanley Creer

Right: With a good head of steam, No 7807 *Compton Manor* climbs Talerddig with a mixed freight, roughly half consisting of empty mineral wagons, during the summer of 1964. *Andrew Muckley*

Left: A Birmingham–Barmouth holiday express, headed by No 7802 *Bradley Manor*, near Talerddig in the summer of 1963. *Ian Allan Library*

Below: Standard Class 4 No 75016 hard at work at the head of the 'Cambrian Coast Express', seen climbing towards Talerddig in September 1966, during the last autumn of operation, before withdrawal at the end of the winter timetable (on 4 March 1967). *Andrew Muckley*

Upper left: Class 2251 0-6-0 No 3200 heads west through Talerddig station on 11 May 1961 with a down freight. Note the presence of the lineside token-exchange equipment and the member of the locomotive crew preparing to exchange tokens for the descent of the bank towards Cemmes Road. *J. R. Besley*

Lower left: No 75002, pictured previously at Talerddig heading a down service on 6 August 1966, had travelled eastwards earlier the same day with a service from Barmouth to Birmingham, being seen here climbing the bank with its eight-coach train. Judging from the amount of smoke, the fireman is working hard to keep the train in motion. *Derek Cross*

Above: Another BR Standard 4-6-0 works hard as it approaches the summit at Talerddig on 23 July 1966. By now the locomotive has been shorn of its smokebox numberplate, indicative of the fact that steam was in decline over the ex-Cambrian lines. *W. Brian Alexander*

Upper right: On 25 May 1964 an up freight trundles through the Dovey Valley headed by 'Manor' 4-6-0 No 7828 *Odney Manor* on the approach to Talerddig Bank. This was the maximum load permitted for an up freight, although the train does contain one unusual element — a bogie coach being used for inspecting the tunnels along the line. *Mark Bourne*

Lower right: With its neighbours Talerddig and Commins Coch Halt, Llanbrynmair was among the stations closed in 1965. Working Timetable Appendices stated that a level crossing which bisected the platform 'must be kept well lighted [sic] after darkness'. Two years before closure No 7828 *Odney Manor* calls with a stopping service for Aberystwyth. *Andrew Muckley*

Upper left: Headed by a Standard Mogul an Aberystwyth-bound stopping train approaches Commins Coch in the summer of 1963. The halt was one of 13 main-line stations and halts between Buttington and Aberystwyth closed in the summer of 1965. *Andrew Muckley*

Lower left: Commins Coch Halt lay amid the rolling, wooded hills between the Severn Valley and the sea. Its 100ft-long platform was under the control of the stationmaster at Cemmes Road, 2¼ miles away, who was instructed to visit the halt from time to time to see that it was kept in proper condition. A view looking west towards the coast in the summer of 1963. *Andrew Muckley*

Right: Standard 2-6-4 tank No 80132 calls at Commins Coch Halt with a morning all-stations service to Aberystwyth in the late summer of 1964. Enginemen found the cabs were snug in winter, as did your author when he rode on the morning stopping service from Oswestry to Aberystwyth in 1964. *Andrew Muckley*

Below: The 'Cambrian Coast Express' between Commins Coch and Cemmes Road, headed by a 'Manor' 4-6-0 carrying a headboard, while only a few carriages have nameboards — this was not one of the smartest formations in the Express Link. *Andrew Muckley*

Above: A slightly careworn 'Manor', No 7827 *Lydham Manor*, heads east through the Dovey Valley at Cemmes Road with a service from Aberystwyth to Shrewsbury on 4 June 1964. *Derek Cross*

Below: The up 'Cambrian Coast Express' (dep Aberystwyth 9.50am, arr Paddington 4pm) near Cemmes Road in August 1964. A dirty No 7819 *Hinton Manor* carries an express headcode but no nameboard. Cemmes Road was the junction for Dinas Mawddwy, terminus of one of the highly individual private railways which added such charm to remote Welsh railways until it became an early casualty of Nationalisation, closing in the autumn of 1950. *Andrew Muckley*

Above: One of the 'Manor' 4-6-0s so familiar on the Cambrian line heads west through the Dovey Valley towards Machynlleth on 26 June 1965. *D. H. Cape*

Below: The 'Cambrian Coast Express' enters Machynlleth on 7 July 1962 behind '43xx' 2-6-0 No 6395. The train split here with portions for Aberystwyth and Pwllheli. *John Scrace*

Above: 'Manor' No 7823 *Hook Norton Manor* enters Machynlleth station with the 'Cambrian Coast Express' for Aberystwyth and Pwllheli on 11 July 1962. The down service divided at Machynlleth, with sections heading north and south from Dovey Junction. *R. F. Roberts*

Below: Changing crew outside Machynlleth signalbox. No 7828 *Odney Manor* after arrival with a stopping train for Aberystwyth in August 1964. *Andrew Muckley*

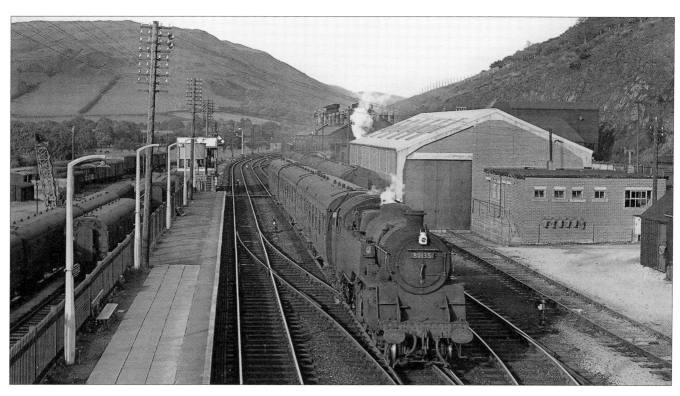

Above: On 28 August 1963 BR Standard 2-6-4T No 80135 brings
empty stock into Machynlleth station to form a service to Aberystwyth.
The locomotive shed, featured below, can be seen in the background.
D. J. Wall

Below: Machynlleth in May 1953, with 'Dukedog' 4-4-0 No 9014 on the
noon Aberystwyth–Whitchurch service and No 9003 in a siding by the
turntable. Note the well-preserved grounded coach body (foreground),
the roofs of coaches in sidings adjacent to the goods yard, and the
former Corris station at a lower level than the main line. *R. W. Miller*

Above: Caught in evening sunshine at
Machynlleth: ex-GWR 0-6-0 No 2268 on an
all-stations Shrewsbury–Aberystwyth service,
allowed more than three hours for the 81-mile
journey, which included nearly 20 stops.
Andrew Muckley

Left: Contrasting starkly with the dignified
station building is the rather ugly standard WR
design of signalbox built at Machynlleth to
replace the East and West 'boxes and seen
nearing completion in the autumn of 1959.
R. A. Savill

Above right: A freshly cleaned No 7819
Hinton Manor gave prestige and importance
to the up 'CCE', when seen approaching
Machynlleth on 29 August 1963.
Andrew Muckley

Lower right: Machynlleth remains the
busiest station on the Cambrian of today,
while Dovey Junction, a lonely outpost on
the marshes of the estuary 4 miles away, is
the junction for the coast line. From platform
ends, generations of enthusiasts loved to
watch the arrival of trains from Aberystwyth
and Barmouth, their progress marked by thin
trails of steam. No 7812 *Erlestoke Manor*
awaits departure with the 6pm Aberystwyth–
Shrewsbury service on 10 May 1965.
R. F. Roberts

Above: One of the remote junctions for which the Cambrian was famous, Dovey Junction was the point where the route divided. To the north, services headed towards Barmouth, and, to the south, towards Aberystwyth. On 18 July 1963 BR Standard 2-6-4T No 80070 heads into the station with a service from Machynlleth to Pwllheli. *P. J. Lynch*

Left: The signalbox at Dovey Junction, seen in the final years before radio signalling, was of standard Western Region design — functional yet rather ugly, and hardly in keeping with the rural charm of the isolated platforms. *Ian Allan Library*

Above right: Four of the main-line economies in June 1965 were of stations between Dovey Junction and Aberystwyth. Only Borth survives. Less than a mile west of Dovey Junction was Glandyfi, within sight of the estuary. The nameboard also stated 'for Llyfnant Valley' — a subtitle not found in public timetables or in the Railway Clearing House Hand-Book of Stations. This was the view towards Dovey Junction in August 1963. *Andrew Muckley*

Right: 'Manor' No 7819 *Hinton Manor* sweeps through Glandyfi at the head of the up 'Cambrian Coast Express' from Aberystwyth on 12 September 1964. *J. C. Beckett*

Above: Glandyfi station closed with effect from on 14 June 1965. In 1964, shortly before closure, 'Manor' No 7821 *Ditcheat Manor* approaches the station from the south with a stopping service from Aberystwyth to Shrewsbury. *M. Dunnett*

Below: Among minor improvements introduced by the Western Region soon after Nationalisation was making Ynyslas a 'set down only' stop for passengers on the early-evening Aberystwyth–Whitchurch local service; previously Ynyslas was the only station between Aberystwyth and Dovey Junction not served by this train. No 7827 *Lydham Manor* arrives with an up service in the summer of 1963. *Andrew Muckley*

Above: Borth is the only station between Dovey Junction and Aberystwyth to remain open. Standard 2-6-4 tank No 80135 prepares to start the 1-in-75 climb to Llandre, over which two-mile section trains were often banked, in August 1964. *Andrew Muckley*

Below: Llandre was a wayside station in the hills some six miles from Aberystwyth. No 7822 *Foxcote Manor* was more than adequate motive power for this train of two corridor coaches bound for Aberystwyth on 29 August 1963. *Andrew Muckley*

Above: Aberystwyth was linked to Carmarthen by three weekday trains taking about 2hr 30min to cover the 56 miles via Pencader and trains generally left from the platform far left in the 'Manchester & Milford'

bay at Aberystwyth (as it was known locally). Here, the bay is being used for the 6.20pm Mail and Passenger train to Whitchurch on 13 August 1961 with No. 7819 *Hinton Manor* at the head. *E. Frangleton*

Right: The Carmarthen branch closed in 1964, and later the Vale of Rheidol terminus at Aberystwyth was switched into the Carmarthen bay, narrow-gauge rails being laid between the platforms with ground-level access for passengers (the original ones being too high to be adapted). The work is seen in progress in May 1968. *R. F. Roberts*

Opposite page, top: Following the end of main-line steam on the Cambrian in 1967 Aberystwyth shed took on a new lease of life, being converted to house the VoR locomotive fleet. Another view of work in May 1968. *R. F. Roberts*

Above left: Some of the most extensive track alterations during BR days took place at Aberystwyth following the closure of the Manchester & Milford and the switching of the narrow-gauge Vale of Rheidol lines to the main station. *R. W. Miller collection*

Above right: There was no better place than the footplate from which to appreciate the steep, curving embankment on the climb out of Aberystwyth towards Borth. This bright wintry scene was captured from the cab of No 7800 *Torquay Manor* on the mid-day up express in January 1964. *Author*

Left: An HST arriving at Aberystwyth during the Mid Wales Festival of Transport in June 1983. *R. W. Miller*

2. THE COAST LINE

Few lines in Britain have been threatened with closure so many times and yet survived. In 1967 — four years after publication of the Beeching Report — it was announced that the coast line, stretching 53 miles from Dovey Junction to Pwllheli, was not among the 3,000 miles of Beeching-threatened lines which the Government was proposing to retain as part of the basic national network. The immediate outcry was so fierce that Transport Minister Barbara Castle ordered a full cost/benefit study of the line. The result, published in late 1969, was not welcomed by the protesters, but in January 1971 notices were posted stating that train services would be withdrawn from 4 October. All stations then open except Towyn, Barmouth and Pwllheli were converted to unstaffed halts used by 'pay trains' manned by conductor-guards.

Reprieve of the line came in 1974, the Government stating that it would stay open because buses could not provide a satisfactory service. But discontent continued, and in 1975 a local MP claimed that the coast line had the slowest passenger services in Britain, with speeds of just over 27mph — 12mph slower than those on the Cambrian main line. The battle to save freight services (which had started before the last steam-hauled freight ran at Christmas 1966) continued for years; as the decline accelerated, local traders and coal merchants in the small towns and villages fought hard to delay withdrawal.

A second major threat which BR's critics thought might give an excuse for closure came in 1980 with the discovery of serious damage to Barmouth Bridge, caused by shipworm. It was closed for emergency repairs and when it reopened on 22 May 1981 it was only to DMUs, with the result that excursion traffic and freight ceased.

The line continued to receive financial support from local authorities, as well as the Government, and in 1984 the Cambrian Coast Line Action Group was given a financial guarantee by Gwynedd County Council towards hiring trains from BR to run services on Sundays in July and August. But there were problems. One of the first such trains was poorly supported, officials stating that people had not wanted to travel because the day was too hot. Barmouth Bridge was reopened to locomotive-hauled trains in May 1986, and in 1987 steam returned to the coast for the first time in 20 years to operate a summer service — the 'Cardigan Bay Express' — linking Machynlleth, Aberystwyth and Barmouth on weekdays and extending to Pwllheli on three Sundays, the trains being timed to enable day-trippers to make a return journey.

Below: Nearly six hours after leaving Paddington, the Pwllheli portion of the 'Cambrian Coast Express' reaches Dovey Junction in late September 1961 behind Standard 2-6-2 tank No 82021. Passengers for Pwllheli faced another 2½ hours of travel. *R. F. Roberts*

Upper right: A Metro-Cammell DMU calls at Dovey Junction on 10 May 1967; despite the destination blind, this is the 10.54 *from* Pwllheli. DMUs began public workings on the main and coast lines in January 1965, running to steam timings. *R. F. Roberts*

Lower right: Ex-GWR Prairie tank No 4549 stands at the sharply curved coast-line platform at Dovey Junction in the summer of 1954 with the 10.45am Machynlleth–Barmouth local service, which connected with the 10.45am from Aberystwyth. At this time the coast line service was the last of the WR services shown in Bradshaw's; immediately following were the Southern Region Eastern Section timetables for another holiday coast — Kent. *R. F. Roberts*

Above: Abertafol, seven miles from Dovey Junction, was one of three halts opened by the GWR between Dovey Junction and Aberdovey. With Gogarth, it was closed in May 1984. *R. F. Roberts*

Right: Penhelig, the most westerly of the three halts, remains open as a request stop; timetables warn passengers that they must hand-signal drivers. This is the view towards Dovey Junction, recorded in May 1967. *R. F. Roberts*

Left: Aberdovey station, where holidaymakers arrived to sample what the last GWR 'Holiday Haunts' guide in 1947 described as 'an unconventional little seaside resort'. *R. F. Roberts*

Upper right: Mogul No 6315 leaves Towyn with the early-afternoon all-stations Barmouth–Machynlleth service in the summer of 1962. It was booked 1hr 17min for the 25½ miles, including nine intermediate stations and two conditional stops. Today's DMUs take nearly 30min less, with eight intermediate station calls possible, though half are conditional. *R. F. Roberts*

Centre right: On 6 September 1962 '2251' 0-6-0 No 2271 shunts the yard at Towyn. One of a batch of 10 built at Swindon in August and September 1934 (to Lot 283), it was in the twilight of its career and would be withdrawn shortly after this photograph was taken. *P. H. Wells*

Below: A reminder that 'Sprinter' trains were to be introduced on the Cambrian from 12 May 1986 was provided by an advertisement in the Talyllyn Railway's 1986 timetables. *Author's collection*

LOCATION MAP

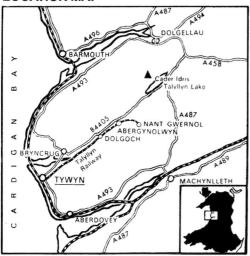

The Talyllyn Railway is a narrow gauge line using steam locomotives on all advertised passenger trains. It was opened in 1865 and runs inland from Tywyn (on the shores of Cardigan Bay), to Nant Gwernol. Much of the railway lies within the Snowdonia National Park and extensive forest walks are available at Nant Gwernol. Tywyn is within easy reach of Aberystwyth and Cambrian Coast Line stations by means of British Rail services.

British Rail's new Sprinter trains commence operation on the Cambrian Lines as from May 12. Through bookings to Nant Gwernol from Shrewsbury, Newtown, Machynlleth, Aberystwyth, Barmouth and Pwllheli.
Enquire locally for fares and train times.

SNOWDONIA NATIONAL PARK GUIDED WALKS IN NANT GWERNOL AREA.

TUESDAYS, JULY 22 TO AUGUST 26

PLEASE ENQUIRE FOR DETAILS

TALYLLYN RAILWAY WHARF STATION, TYWYN, GWYNEDD LL36 9EY   Telephone: TYWYN (0654) 710472

Above: A DMU pauses at Llwyngwril with a morning Pwllheli–Machynlleth service in the spring of 1968. The substantial platform buildings of this isolated station act as a reminder that, for a brief period in the 1860s, this was the terminus of the coast line. *R. F. Roberts*

Left: Steam haulage through Friog, Britain's only railway avalanche shelter: No 7819 *Hinton Manor* heads the 'Cardigan Bay Express' in June 1987. 'The passage round the headland of Friog is spectacular indeed,' stated a 'Welcome Back Barmouth Bridge' publicity leaflet in April 1986. *R. W. Miller*

Above: Viewed looking northwards at Fairbourne, '43xx' Mogul No 6395 is seen at the head of the 3.25pm service from Barmouth to Machynlleth on 10 July 1962. *John Scrace*

Left: In 1962 a small batch of Standard 2-6-4 tanks was transferred from the London, Tilbury & Southend section to work lines in mid-Wales from several sheds, including Machynlleth and Oswestry. No 80104 heads an up freight through Fairbourne in May 1965. *R. F. Roberts*

Right: For some three decades camping coaches were sited in sidings at a number of stations. Coach M021693M, one of the last survivors, was recorded at Fairbourne in the summer of 1968. Three years later the London Midland Region removed camping coaches from Llwyngwril, Fairbourne, Aberdovey and Borth; by then the popularity of camping coaches was in sharp decline. *R. F. Roberts*

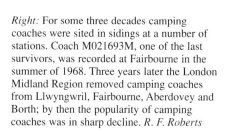

Above: When Barmouth Junction was renamed Morfa Mawddach, in June 1960, it retained its large and informative nameboard, but this fell out of use some five years later after the closure of the route through the Dee Valley from Ruabon. *R. F. Roberts*

Centre left: Barmouth was linked to North West England by four weekday trains through the Dee Valley. There were also Summer Saturday extras and here '22xx' 0-6-0 No 2247 and an unidentified sister double-head one of these, a Manchester-Pwllheli extra, away from Barmouth Junction on 10 August 1957. The train joined Cambrian metals at Dolgelley. *R. E. Vincent*

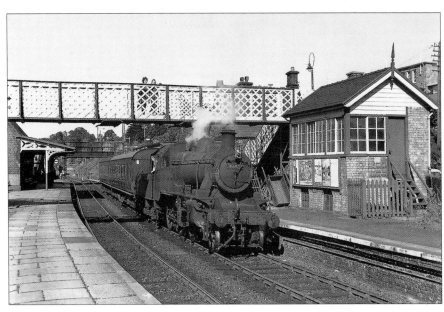

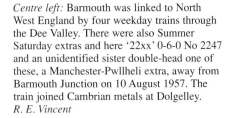

Lower left: The Morfa Mawddach–Dolgellau stretch ran for almost eight miles through delightful scenery beside the Mawddach estuary. Always regarded as part of the GWR Ruabon–Barmouth route, it was Cambrian-owned until Grouping. This scene was recorded at Dolgellau in the early 1960s, showing the original Cambrian platform building (*left*). *R. W. Miller collection*

CROESO' N ÔL BONT Y BERMO
WELCOME BACK BARMOUTH BRIDGE
13 APRIL 1986

Rheilffordd y Cambrian
The Cambrian Railway

Above: Steam returned to the Cambrian for the first time in 20 years with the launch in 1987 of the 'Cardigan Bay Express', a summer service between Machynlleth, Aberystwyth and Pwllheli. The inaugural working, hauled by No 7819 *Hinton Manor*, crosses Barmouth Bridge on 24 May. *British Rail*

Below: The third locomotive, replacing No 75069, to work the 'Cardigan Bay Express' was Mogul No 46443, seen with a good head of steam on a return working at Barmouth on 12 August 1987. *R. W. Miller*

Right: The up 'Cambrian Coast Express' leaves Barmouth on the morning of Monday 22 August 1966, with 4-6-0s Nos 75052 and 75040. The second locomotive was returning home after a Saturday-only working. *R. W. Miller*

Below: Steam returned to the Cambrian amid a great flourish of publicity in the summer of 1987 with the 'Cardigan Bay Express'. The service ran between Machynlleth, Aberystwyth and Barmouth Monday–Friday and along the coast line on three Sundays. Leaflets warned passengers that it might be necessary to substitute diesel traction if fire risk developed. *Author's collection*

BRITISH RAILWAYS

NEW FOR 1987 . . . . .
THE CARDIGAN BAY EXPRESS

Steam on the Cambrian Coast Line
Machynlleth to Barmouth,
Aberystwyth and Pwllheli

SUMMER 1987

Rheilffordd y Cambrian
Cambrian Coast Line

Centre right: Locomotive variety at Barmouth, as three types meet in April 1962. Pannier No 7442 and Standard 2-6-2 tank No 82021 wait in the Ruabon bay, south of the main station as No 7811 *Dunley Manor* leaves with the 3.25pm to Wrexham. *J. F. Ward*

Right: BR Standard 4-6-0 No 75020 departs from Barmouth with the 3.25pm service to Machynlleth on 20 July 1962. *John Scrace*

Left: Standard 4-6-0 No 75002 passes Barmouth South 'box as a token is exchanged. The 'box is a Dutton design of a type found on several parts of the Cambrian. *R. W. Miller*

Right: A busy summer scene at Barmouth on 29 July 1963, with Standard tank No 82020 departing northwards along the coast. Visible in the background are three other steam locomotives — a second 2-6-2 tank opposite the 'box, another in the distance behind it and a fourth tank attached to carriages to the right of the 'box. *R. W. Miller*

Below: BR Standard 2-6-4T No 80097 departs northwards from Llanbedr & Pensarn with the 6pm service from Barmouth to Pwllheli on 11 September 1964. *J. C. Beckett*

Above: The GWR introduced the '2251' class of 0-6-0s in 1930, but it was another eight years before the type was seen on the Cambrian main line. Between 1946 and 1959 some 16 of the class were so employed, but by 1963 their ranks had been reduced to just three, including No 2255, seen at Harlech in April 1961. *R. F. Roberts*

Right: The proposed closure of the coast line in the early 1970s was so strongly opposed locally that the Government was forced to order a second public inquiry, held at Harlech in February 1972, to investigate alternative bus services. *Author's collection*

Below: On 22 April 1963 BR Standard Class 2 2-6-2T No 82034 arrives at Minffordd with a southbound local service. The Ffestiniog Railway station serving the town is located slightly to the east of this point, the Cambrian being crossed by the narrow-gauge line by means of an overbridge. *M. R. C. Price*

CAMBRIAN COAST LINE RAILWAY
DYFI JUNCTION to PWLLHELI

IN JUNE 1971, A 2-DAY PUBLIC INQUIRY LOOKED INTO THE PROPOSED CLOSURE OF THIS RAILWAY.

1—The Transport Users' Consultative Committee for Wales, who conducted the Inquiry, reported unanimously that "WIDESPREAD HARDSHIP" would follow closure of this line.

2—There was clear evidence (the TUCC said) "THAT THERE WERE NO OTHER PRACTICAL MEANS OF TRANSPORT AVAILABLE IN THE AREA."

3—The Welsh Council strongly and unequivocally opposed closure.

4—Every interested organisation opposed closure.

5—All elected representatives of the people of this area opposed closure.

6—Over 10,000 people signed (mainly on the trains) a petition opposing closure.

Peter Walker, Secretary of State for the Environment, **IS NOT SATISFIED ! !**

He has called another **INQUIRY** at the **MEMORIAL HALL, HARLECH, 10 a.m., WEDNESDAY, 9th FEBRUARY, 1972.** This is to investigate alternative bus services.

THIS IS A FARCICAL SUGGESTION !

O By BUS—JOURNEY TIMES much longer than by train.

O By BUS—COST MUCH HIGHER.

Fairbourne to Barmouth by Train, 2 miles; only possible Bus route, 18 miles ! !

OPPOSE THIS EXPENSIVE NONSENSE !

WE SAY:

1—The area NEEDS the line.

2—Properly run, the line could be run with a MUCH SMALLER SUBSIDY.

3—Bus services would need subsidies anyway.

4—No guarantee bus services would run for more than about two years.

5—Set up a Transport Co-ordinating Committee to integrate rail and remaining bus services.

6—If you haven't already told the Transport Users' Consultative Committee of your objections (the hardship) to alternative bus services, contact us and we'll present your case.

7—ATTEND THE INQUIRY IF AT ALL POSSIBLE. ((Train times available at stations).

IF WE FAIL, THE LINE COULD CLOSE THIS YEAR ! !

For further information contact—The Secretary, Cambrian Coast Line Action Group, 12 Corbett Close, TYWYN, Meirionnydd

PASS THIS LEAFLET ON TO A FRIEND

Y Dydd Press Ltd., Dolgellau (Tel. 547)

Above: Beyond Cambrian boundaries. As well as publicising the Class 150 'Sprinters' introduced the previous summer, the bilingual 1987 summer timetable gave timings of long-distance through services to the West Midlands, Euston (and Paddington with a change at Birmingham New Street), Chester and Shrewsbury. On the coast line, Minffordd was 'for Ffestiniog Railway'. *Author's collection*

Above right: Minffordd provides a useful interchange between the standard- and narrow-gauge lines. In the summer of 1988 a return excursion from Pwllheli picks up passengers from the Ffestiniog Railway. The locomotive is Class 37/4 No 37429 *Eisteddfod Genedlaethol. R. W. Miller*

Centre right: In August 1976 — two decades after the revived Ffestiniog Railway reached Minffordd — *Linda* stands on the bridge spanning the coast line and station, with its derelict signalbox. *R. W. Miller*

Right: The small group of goods and slate sidings at Minffordd had a single connection to the coast line from the direction of Penrhyndeudraeth. They were difficult to work because of a falling gradient of 1 in 50, and staff were told to use sprags if necessary, to make sure wagons standing on the main line during shunting operations did not move. BR Type 2 diesel No D5084 shunts in the spring of 1967. *R. F. Roberts*

Above: A four-car DMU formation awaits departure from Porthmadog as the 3.45pm to Barmouth in May 1966. The service, which ran only during term-time, was booked to take 60 minutes for the 19-mile journey, including 12 stops, half of them at halts. *R. F. Roberts*

Below: Two Cambrian goods brake vans were still running in 1959. Double-ended No W8794 (Cambrian No 11) was at Portmadoc 'NOT IN COMMON USE'; it was also labelled 'PORTMADOC RU' (restricted use). *Ian Allan Library*

Upper right: The 'Cardigan Bay Express', with which (stated British Railways) steam was coming back to the coast line in style, ran to leisurely timetables in 1987 to give passengers time to enjoy some of the finest of Britain's coastal scenery. The journey from Machynlleth to Pwllheli took just over 2½ hours, including a 20-minute stop at Barmouth. On the return leg this was extended to nearly an hour. Bound for Pwllheli, No 7819 *Hinton Manor* arrives at Porthmadog on 9 August. *R. W. Miller*

Centre right: Locomotive crews working the 'Cardigan Bay Express' between Machynlleth and Pwllheli, which ran on three Sundays in the summer of 1987, faced tender-first return runs of nearly 60 miles — hardly what sturdy 4-6-0s were designed for. On 9 August No 7819 *Hinton Manor* departs from Porthmadog, which, with Barmouth and Tywyn, was one of only three intermediate stops. *R. W. Miller*

Right: 'Dukedog' No 9021 heads a southbound freight through Portmadoc during the mid-1950s. *A. J. Clarke*

Above: Black Rock Halt, between Porthmadog and Criccieth, was one of the most remote on the coast line. Its closure by the London Midland Region on safety grounds on 13 August 1976 was confirmed as permanent by the Department of Transport almost a year later, on 27 June 1977. *R. W. Miller*

LONDON AND CAMBRIAN COAST

(Timetable summarising services to/from the Cambrian Coast, showing columns for the 'Cambrian Coast Express' and 'The Welshman'. The table is arranged in four panels: Paddington to Aberystwyth, Aberystwyth to Paddington, Paddington to Pwllheli, and Pwllheli to Paddington, with WEEK DAYS and SUNDAYS sections.)

Notes:

A Seats can be reserved in advance on payment of a fee of 2s. 0d. per seat (see page 49)

a am

AB Automatic Buffet between Shrewsbury and Aberystwyth in each direction

B Conveys 1st and 2nd class Sleeping Car (limited accommodation) between Paddington and Gobowen

b On Saturdays arr 6 minutes *earlier*

C Conveys 1st and 2nd class Sleeping Car (limited accommodation) between Paddington and Carmarthen

c On Saturdays arrives 4 minutes earlier

D On Saturdays dep Barmouth 2 20 pm, Dolgellau 2 50 pm and arr London (Paddington) 10 14 pm

d On Saturdays arr 1 40 pm

E Except Saturdays

EG Except Saturdays runs 1st July to 30th August inclusive

f Applies until 31st August inclusive

g On Saturdays arrives 1 10 pm

H Via Ruabon

h On Saturdays arr 8 13 pm

J Via Gobowen and Oswestry

K Via Gobowen, Oswestry and Machynlleth

k On Sats. arr 1 11 pm

L On Saturdays arr 2 11 pm

M Conveys 1st and 2nd class Sleeping Car (limited accommodation) between Paddington and Ruabon

m Via Crewe and Bangor

MB Miniature Buffet Car provided in some cases for a portion of the journey only

N Via Dovey Junc. Second class only to Morfa Mawddach

n Via Bangor and Crewe

P Limited accommodation. Reserved seat passengers only. Note "A" applies. Seats must be claimed at least 10 minutes before the advertised departure time

Q Arrives London (St. Pancras)

RB Buffet Car provided in some cases for a portion of the journey only

RC Restaurant Car provided, in some cases for a portion of the journey only

RX RC and MB Mondays to Fridays. RB Saturdays only

S Saturdays only

T Commences 29th June

u Calls when required to take up passengers

V Via Carmarthen

W For Pwllheli Holiday Camp

Y Via Carmarthen. On Saturdays dep 12 0 noon

Z Conveys 1st and 2nd class Sleeping Car (limited accommodation) between Paddington and Shrewsbury

HEAVY FIGURES INDICATE THROUGH CARRIAGES FROM OR TO LONDON

Right: In the 1950s, when roads to the coast were becoming congested because of the popularity of holiday motoring, the London Midland Region and, later, the Western Region introduced Land Cruises from Llandudno and other coastal resorts in North Wales. These were immediately popular, and three cruises ran on some days. They followed roundabout routes, all including Barmouth–Afonwen. *Author's collection*

Left: Timetable summarising services to/from the Cambrian Coast in the summer of 1963. Adjacent columns showed two titled trains-the 'Welshman' and 'Cambrian Coast Express'. *Ian Allan Library*

Above: The most northerly junction of the coast line was at Afon Wen, with the branch from Bangor. This busy scene, recorded during the summer of 1952, depicts Fairburn 2-6-4T No 42260 reversing with the 3.30pm Pwllheli–Llandudno Junction, while on the far left is Mogul No 46430 with a Land Cruise excursion. Note the fine array of signals dominating this isolated junction. *J. A. Peden*

Below: Afon Wen Junction, as the station nameboard proudly proclaims, was the point where the ex-LMS line to Caernarvon (as then spelled) and Bangor headed northwards. On 9 August 1948, shortly after Nationalisation, LMS 2-6-4T No 2258 awaits departure with the 10.55am service to Bangor, alongside GWR '45xx' 2-6-2T No 4560 at the head of the 8.15am service from Machynlleth to Pwllheli. The line from Afon Wen to Caernarfon would lose its passenger services from 7 December 1964. *SLS collection*

Upper left: The Pwllheli portion of the 'Cambrian Coast Express' passing Afon Wen in May 1964 behind 0-6-0 No 3208. The junction, at which the express was not scheduled to call, would close the following December, together with the line north as far as Caernarvon. *R. F. Roberts*

Lower left: One of the most substantial of Cambrian 'boxes, Pwllheli West was brick-built and slate-roofed, with finials and decorative barge boards. *Ian Allan Library*

Above: The long and broad island platform at Pwllheli has been reduced to a single face — hardly an imposing or welcoming terminus for so spectacular a route. This was the scene in May 1966. *R. F. Roberts*

Right: A through service from Swansea (High Street) to Butlin's at Pwllheli included a 32min wait for passengers from Newport and Cardiff changing at Swansea. The total journey time could be 9½ hours. In 1959 the service was restricted to summer Saturdays between mid-June and August. *Author's collection*

WESTERN   **BRITISH RAILWAYS**   REGION

THROUGH TRAIN SERVICE
Swansea, Llanelly, Carmarthen, Aberystwyth, Barmouth and Penychain (BUTLIN'S HOLIDAY CAMP)

WITH CONNECTIONS FROM AND TO OTHER SOUTH WALES STATIONS

SATURDAYS ONLY

SUMMER, 1959

JUNE 20th TO AUGUST 29th (incl.)			JUNE 27th TO SEPTEMBER 5th (incl.)		
NEWPORT		a.m.			a.m.
CARDIFF (General)	dep.	7 32	PWLLHELI	dep.	10A 0
BRIDGEND	"	8 0	PENYCHAIN	"	10 18
PORT TALBOT (General)	"	8 32	AFON WEN	"	10 23
BRITON FERRY	"	9 0	CRICCIETH	"	10 33
NEATH (General)	"	9 8	PORTMADOC	"	10 43
SWANSEA (High Street)	arr.	9 38	HARLECH	"	11 0
			BARMOUTH	arr.	11 23
		a.m.		dep.	11 28
SWANSEA (High Street)	dep.	10 10			p.m.
COCKETT	"	10 20	TOWYN	"	12 2
GOWERTON (North)	"	10 25	ABERDOVEY	"	12 12
LOUGHOR	"	10 30	ABERYSTWYTH	arr.	1 20
LLANELLY	"	10 40		dep.	1 45
PEMBREY & BURRY PORT	"	10 49	LAMPETER	"	2 49
KIDWELLY	"	10 58	PENCADER	"	3 16
FERRYSIDE	"	11 6	CARMARTHEN	arr.	3 55
CARMARTHEN	arr.	11 20			
	dep.	11 35			
		p.m.	CARMARTHEN	dep.	4 10
PENCADER	"	12 14	FERRYSIDE	arr.	4 22
LAMPETER	"	12 39	KIDWELLY	"	4 30
ABERYSTWYTH	arr.	1 35	PEMBREY & BURRY PORT	"	4 39
	dep.	1 40	LLANELLY	"	4 50
ABERDOVEY	"	2 48	LOUGHOR	"	4 57
TOWYN	"	2 58	GOWERTON (North)	"	5 2
BARMOUTH	arr.	3 40	COCKETT	"	5 10
	dep.	3 46	SWANSEA (High Street)	"	5 18
HARLECH	arr.	4 8	NEATH (General)	"	5 45
PORTMADOC	"	4 28	BRITON FERRY	"	6B37
CRICCIETH	"	4 44	PORT TALBOT (General)	"	6 0
AFON WEN	"	4 51	BRIDGEND	"	6 20
PENYCHAIN	"	4 56	CARDIFF (General)	"	6 52
PWLLHELI	"	5 5	NEWPORT	"	7 17

A—Change at Afon Wen.   B—Change at Swansea (High Street).

Paddington Station, W.2.
April, 1959.

J. R. HAMMOND, General Manager.

Printed in Great Britain by C. E. Watkins Ltd., Green Dragon Lane, Swansea.   T.E. 1476

3. THE MID-WALES RAILWAY

Fourteen years after Nationalisation the busy and strategically placed small town of Brecon was wiped off the railway map of Britain by the closure of four routes. First to go was Brecon–Neath (Riverside), on 15 October 1962. It was followed only a few weeks later, on 31 December, by the others — Brecon–Newport, Hereford–Hay–Brecon and, longest of all, the 60 miles of the Mid-Wales Railway route from Moat Lane to Brecon. Altogether they caused the loss of about 350 railway jobs and resulted in the total closure of some 170 miles of railway. Following a public enquiry the TUCC for Wales & Monmouthshire stated that, if hardship was to be minimised, new bus services must be provided over the full routes of the Mid-Wales and Hereford–Brecon lines.

The Mid-Wales Railway once personified the Cambrian's inland section, winding through the rolling hills of the Wye and neighbouring valleys serving small but busy market towns. It was,

loosely, a through route to the Cambrian coast for holidaymakers, tourists and commercial travellers to/from South Wales, who changed at Moat Lane Junction. The Stephenson Locomotive Society (SLS) marked its passing in 'Camwell' style, with a packed double-headed eight-coach corridor special, run on the last Sunday of the year, which made a round trip from Shrewsbury via Hereford. An abiding memory that has remained with your author for more than 40 years is of passengers enjoying cups of tea in the brake van. They were surprised and grateful, yet angry that tea was something they had never been able to enjoy through the years they travelled on the line. The glory of snow-covered fields added poignancy and sadness to the day and left some passengers wondering why there was any need to close the line.

Several months after closure Llanidloes Borough Council asked a group of Welsh MPs to assist in retaining the trackbed.

They agreed but pointed out they had been informed by the Ministry of Transport that it was satisfied that the line had no strategic importance and that there was no point in retaining a long stretch of track through sparsely populated countryside.

In the mid-1970s there was another battle, this time successful, to save the historic and imposing station at Llanidloes, when this was threatened with demolition as the trackbed was swallowed up by a by-pass to carry traffic on the main road to/from South Wales clear of Llanidloes.

Below: Moat Lane Junction, some four miles south of Newtown, closed when passenger services over the Mid-Wales Railway to Brecon ceased at the end of 1962, but the main-line platform continued to be used by Oswestry–Aberystwyth stopping trains, although they called only for water. On a crisp January morning in 1964, Standard 2-6-4 tank No 80131 (on which your author was cab-riding), was allowed six minutes. The imposing three-storey station, set in the middle of fields, is in the background (*right*). *Author*

Right: The imposing station at Llanidloes was built in the early 1860s as a joint facility for three railway companies — the Llanidloes & Newtown, the Mid-Wales and the Manchester & Milford. Some 90 years later, in May 1954, Mogul No 46517 calls with a stopping service from Brecon. The train would terminate at Moat Lane, where, within a few minutes, passengers could catch connecting trains for Whitchurch or Aberystwyth.
R. W. Miller

Left: The snowy scene at Llanidloes as the last train from Moat Lane to Brecon, an SLS special, pauses for a photo stop on 30 December 1962. Subsequently the area changed out of all recognition; although the station building was preserved following a public enquiry, the rest was swallowed up by a by-pass to carry the busy South Wales trunk road clear of the town. *Author*

Right: Looking south from Llanidloes, where engine crews began an unbroken stiff climb of several miles to the 947ft line summit at Pantydwr. The last special of eight corridor coaches was double-headed. *Author*

FAREWELL TO THE BRECON LINES
OF THE FORMER CAMBRIAN AND MIDLAND RAILWAYS

W. A. Camwell
Photo:
G.W.R. 896, ex Cambrian Railways, on the 2-40 p.m. Moat Lane—Brecon,
entering Newbridge on Wye on 15th September, 1949.

Photographic Souvenir
in connection with the

LAST PASSENGER TRAIN
on the

Moat Lane to Brecon and Brecon to Hereford lines
SUNDAY, 30th DECEMBER, 1962.

Organised by the
STEPHENSON LOCOMOTIVE SOCIETY
(Midland Area)

Left: A footnote in Bradshaw's stated that Newbridge-on-Wye was '4½ miles to Llandrindod Wells Station'. There was a similar note in Bradshaw's Central Wales-line timetables. Today only Builth Road (minus the 'High Level' suffix) survives, as a request stop. *Author's collection*

Above: Builth Road Low Level. The large nameboard advised passengers to change for several stations on the Central Wales line — Llandrindod, Llanwrtyd Wells and its neighbour, Llangammarch Wells.
R. F. Roberts

Above: Builth Road Low Level in the summer of 1959, looking south towards Three Cocks Junction. 'Low Level' was added as late as 1950, the Central Wales-line station being suffixed 'High Level'. Today it survives as a request stop, called simply 'Builth Road'. *R. F. Roberts*

Right: As well as a short, curved track spur there was a luggage lift and a wide passenger footpath between the Builth Road platforms. Public timetables showed that passenger trains on both lines were allowed stops of several minutes. *R. F. Roberts*

Below: Builth Road Low Level station, dating from Cambrian days, was quickly converted to agricultural use after the Mid-Wales Railway closed, the trackbed providing easy access. *Author*

Below: The ex-LMS 2-6-0s designed by Ivatt became a familiar sight on the Cambrian during the final years of steam operation. Two are pictured at Three Cocks Junction in 1962: that on the left has arrived from Moat Lane and will head southwards to Talyllyn Junction and Brecon, whilst that on the right has arrived over the ex-Midland line from Hereford with a service that will terminate at Three Cocks. By this date services over these lines were living on borrowed time; the route from Moat Lane to Brecon, along with that from Three Cocks to Hereford, would close on 31 December 1962. *Leslie Sandler*

Left: In the years leading to closure a variety of motive power hauled local services, pannier tank No 9674 being seen near Whitney-on-Wye. Trains between Hereford, Hay and Brecon often seemed to have more than adequate accommodation for the generally sparse passenger traffic. *C. R. Berridge*

Right: Routes from Moat Lane, Hereford, Newport and Neath converged at Brecon. Ivatt Mogul No 46521 is seen after arriving with a two-coach service. *Author's collection*

Table 185 **MOAT LANE, LLANIDLOES, BUILTH ROAD, HEREFORD and BRECON**

WEEK DAYS ONLY

Miles	Station	am	am	am		am	am	am	am	am	am	pm		pm	pm	am	pm	pm	pm	pm	pm		pm	pm		pm	pm	pm		pm	pm	pm	pm	pm	
	184Whitchurch dep		3 15													9 45				1 30				1 30						4 30			6 50	6 50	
	184Welshpool „		4 40								8 57					11 20				3 7				4 40						7 18			8 45	1040	
	184Aberystwyth „										7 35					10 30		12 35		2 45				2 45						6 0					
—	Moat Lane Junction dep		5 45			8 30					9 55					12p27		2 50		4 45				5 27						8 3			9 26	1118	
2	Llandinam		5 50			8 35					10 0					12 32		2 55		4 50				5 31						8 8			9 31	1123	
5	Dolwen Halt		dd			8 41					10 6					12 38		dd		4 56				5 37						8 14			9 37	uu	
7¾	Llanidloes arr		6 2			8 46					1012					12 44		3 5		5 2				5 45						8 20			9 42	1133	
	Llanidloes dep		6 5								1015							3 6						5 46											
11	Tylwch Halt		dd								1024							3 13						5 54				Saturdays only					Except Saturdays	Saturdays only	
12½	Glan-yr-afon Halt					Except Saturdays and School Holidays					1029							dd						5S59											
14¾	Pantydwr		6 24								1035							3 30						6 6											
16¼	St. Harmons		dd								1039							3 33						6 10											
19	Marteg Halt										1046							dd						dd											
21½	Rhayader		6 42								1054							3 47					Saturdays only	6 23											
24¾	Doldowlod Halt		6 50								11 1							3 54						6 30											
29	Newbridge-on-Wye F		6 58								11 9							4 2						6 41											
32¾	Builth Road arr		7 6								1117							4 10						6 48											
	(Low Level) dep	6 30	7 7				9 18	9 42			1119				1230			4 11						6 50			8 8								
34½	Builth Wells arr	6 33	7 10				9 23	9 45			1122				1233			4 14						6 54			8 11								
	Builth Wells dep	6 35					9 30				1125				1 20			4 18								Except Saturdays		8 15				Saturdays only			
36½	Llanfaredd Halt						9 35				1129				1 25			dd										uu							
38½	Aberedw	6 44					9 39				1134				1 30			dd										uu							
41¼	Erwood	6 50					9 45				1140				1 35		Except Saturdays and School Holidays	4 29										8 27							
43¼	Llanstephan Halt						9 51				1147				1 41			4 35										uu							
45½	Boughrood and Llyswen	7 0					9 57				1152				1 45			4 40					Commences 11th May, 1963					8 33							
—	Mls Hereford dep								9 2					1242							4 0					7 35						9 10			
—	5 Credenhill								9 13					1255					Saturdays only		4 12														
—	9¼ Moorhampton								9 22					1 4							4 20											9 30			
—	12½ Kinnersley								9 30					1 12							4 28					8 0						9 38			
—	14¼ Eardisley								9 36					1 17							4 34					8 5						9 45			
—	17½ Whitney-on-Wye								9 44					1 24							4 42					8 12						9 52			
—	21½ Hay-on-Wye			7X55					9 54					1 34							5 1					8 25						10 5			
—	25¼ Glasbury-on-Wye			8X 2					10 2					1 43							5 9					8 32						1013			
48½	Three Cocks Junction arr	7 7		8X 7			10 4		10 8		1159			1 48	1 52			4 47			5 14					8 37		8 39				1018			
	Three Cocks Junction dep	7 9		8 8					1012	From Newport (Table 121)	12 0	From Newport (Table 121)			1 55		4 30	4 50	From Newport (Table 121)		5 18		From Pontsticill (Table 121)			8 40		8 40			From Newport (Table 121)	1020			
50½	Talgarth	7 16		8 14					1017		12 6				2 1		4 38	4 56			5P30					8 45		8 45				1025			
53	Trefeinon Halt	7 23		8 20					1024		1213				dd		4 44	dd			dd					8 53		uu				aa			
54¾	Llangorse Lake Halt	7 30		8 24					1029		1218				dd		4 49	5 8			dd					8 57		uu				aa			
56	Talyllyn Junction arr	7 35		8 29					1033		1223				2 16		4 53	5 12			5P46					9 1		8 57				1037			
98½	121Newport arr	10 4									2 48				4 27						8S50														
96¾	121Cardiff D 131 „	1047									3n28				5 6						9 8														
—	Talyllyn Junction dep	7 47		8 31					1036	1046	1225	1 34			2 20		4 54	5 17	5 26		5P47		7 30			9 2		8 58			9 24	1040			
58	Groesffordd Halt	7 52		8 35						1050	1230				2 25		4 58	dd	5 31		dd					9 6		uu			uu				
60	Brecon arr	7 57		8 41					1044	1055	1235	1 42			2 30		5 4	5 25	5 36		5P56		7 38			9 11		9 8			9 33	1050			

aa Calls to take up on notice being given to the Station Master at Talgarth. Passengers wishing to alight must give notice to Guard at Talgarth

D Queen Street, via Bargoed

dd Calls if required on notice to Guard at previous *stopping* station or by giving hand-signal during daylight only

F 4½ miles to Llandrindod Wells Station

n On Saturdays arr 3 6 pm

P 4 minutes later on Saturdays

p pm

S Saturdays only

uu Calls to set down on notice being given to Guard at previous *stopping* station

X Except Saturdays and School Holidays

Above: The Western Region 1962 winter timetable, advertised to be in operation from 10 September until further notice. But table 185 (Moat Lane–Brecon weekday-only service) was deleted after only a few weeks, the line closing after an SLS special, which ran on the last Sunday of the year. *Author's collection*

Lower left: A Moat Lane service, formed of ex-GWR No 2219 and a train of mixed corridor stock, departing Brecon in the spring of 1960. Journey times between Moat Lane and Brecon changed little between Nationalisation and the line's closure at the end of 1962. *R. W. Miller collection*

Above: The last train, seen earlier on page 55, reached Brecon without incident on 30 December 1962 after local police forces had confirmed that no fresh snowfalls were likely in the afternoon. *Author's collection*

4. BRANCH-LINE DECLINE

The year 1965 marked the end of some 15 years in which a number of branch lines of varying length, importance, character and charm, which gave such fascination to the railways of Wales, had been closed completely.

First to go, in the autumn of 1950, was the former Mawddwy Railway, which had lost its passenger services as early as the winter of 1931, though goods trains had continued to trundle almost seven miles up the valley from Cemmes Road to Dinas Mawddwy through peace- and wartime.

The decline of railways around Oswestry was centred on the Tanat Valley, served by a single-line branch from Llynclys Junction, some 3½ miles south, to the village of Llangynog, at the foot of the Berwyn Mountains. The 14 miles stretching from Porthywaen closed to passengers on 15 January 1951. Infrequent weekday trains had taken almost 1¼ hours to cover the 19½-mile journey from Oswestry. One of 10 intermediate stations was Llanrhaiadr Mochnant — hardly convenient for local people, since (as Bradshaw's warned) it was a mile and a half away from the village — which became the freight railhead for the valley after the 5-mile western tip of the line to Llangynog closed in the summer of 1952.

Abermule lingers in the memory of historians and enthusiasts as the scene of the Cambrian's worst disaster rather than as the junction for one of its most remote branches, which climbed nearly four miles into the sheep-rearing hills flanking the main line, to a terminus two miles from the village of Kerry, from which it took its name. Closure proposals were put forward in the mid-1950s and were discussed in two annual reports of the TUCC, which decided it could not agree with representations by local authorities and one man concerned about the movement of corn and fertiliser traffic. Closure, on 1 May 1956, was to goods only, the GWR having withdrawn passenger services with effect from 9 February 1931 — the same day as those on the Welshpool & Llanfair.

Wrexham was the largest town ever served by the Cambrian and was connected to the main line by a 13-mile branch to Ellesmere. Single-coach auto-trains terminated at the small Wrexham Central station (formerly the terminus for LNER stopping trains to/from Seacombe). In the final years before closure, which came in the autumn of 1962, only about 300 passengers a week used the services, which connected at Ellesmere with either Whitchurch or Oswestry trains — sometimes with both. After the last passenger train puffed out of Wrexham Central on 12 September 1962 the *Liverpool Daily Post* reported that it was with all the fuss and excitement of a Sunday school outing to the seaside. But, it added, no-one seemed to mourn the end of this 67-year-old branch.

A gap of 37 years between the withdrawal of the Tanat passenger trains in 1951 and the end of Oswestry–Nantmawr quarry trains in 1988 might sound like a record, but the delay on the half-mile Harbour branch at Aberdovey — the Cambrian's only port — was almost three times as long, the branch closing to passengers in 1867 but staying open for goods for almost a century longer, until the spring of 1964. Once the rails were lifted, the harbourside became a pleasant tourist area with a small maritime museum and National Park centre.

Most southerly of the Oswestry group of branches, with stations on both sides of the Wales/England border, was the 8½-mile single-line branch from Llanymynech to the small market town of Llanfyllin, which closed, with the Welshpool–Whitchurch main line, on 18 January 1965. 'Perhaps the least interesting of Cambrian branches' was how Roger Kidner described it in his Oakwood Press volume *The Cambrian Railways*. Certainly it lacked the charisma of the Tanat, its closest neighbour to the north, because its weekday-only trains were operated by thoroughly modern Standard locomotives and rolling stock; in contrast, those of the Tanat Valley (which ran until 1951) consisted of the smallest and oldest locomotives and coaches.

Discerning enthusiasts single them out as being of especial delight, and the sentimental journeys by enthusiasts no doubt modestly boosted passenger figures. The 'least interesting branch' sentiment may not have been shared by Oliver Veltom, the Divisional Manager held in such high regard both by railwaymen and by the public. When your author lunched with him once at his home in the Vyrnwy Valley he mentioned how he and his wife had drawn the curtains as a mark of respect on the day the Llanfyllin branch closed.

Below: The Dinas Mawddwy Railway (1867) was one of the most charming of Victorian independent railways, being tucked away in the rolling hills behind the coast. Passenger services from Cemmes Road, on the main line, were withdrawn from January 1931, but a diminishing goods service survived for almost two decades, until September 1950. *Author's collection*

Right: The locomotive shed at Dinas Mawddwy viewed in 1949, some 18 years after it had been closed by the Great Western Railway. The first locomotive shed here had been constructed by the Mawddwy Railway and opened on 1 October 1867; this early facility was replaced by the structure shown here in 1911, which was to remain in use until closure on 1 January 1931. It was subsequently used for industrial purposes and was still extant in 1997. *Ian Allan Library*

Above: An interesting panorama of Dinas Mawddwy in August 1939 which illustrates well the relationship between the locomotive shed (on the left), the main station building and the goods shed. By this date the branch was freight-only, having lost its passenger services on 1 January 1931. The original Dinas Mawddwy company ceased operation on 17 April 1901, and it was a decade later, on 31 July 1911, that the line reopened under the ægis of the Cambrian Railways. *SLS collection*

Right: Caersws. The sharply curved one-time terminus of the 6½-mile Van Railway, serving lead mines in the hills, closed to passengers in 1879 but survived into Nationalisation as part of the District Engineer's depot. This was the view, recorded in the summer of 1964, towards the main line, on which Caersws station remains open today, following reprieve from closure in 1965. *Andrew Muckley*

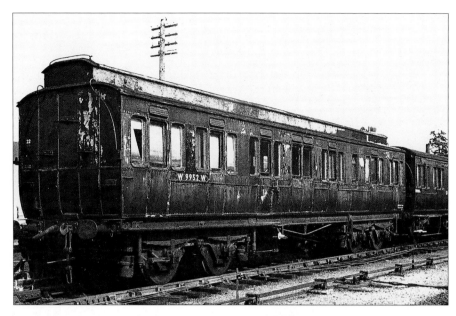

Left: Caersws depot was home — the final home? — of an interesting group of ancient passenger coaches, seen there in 1964. Despite their dilapidated appearance they were in serviceable condition, judging from instructions clearly painted on the outside to 'shunt with care'. Largest was eight-wheel clerestory W9952, a former Camping Coach converted to a Mess Van, here standing next to an ex-GWR four-wheeler. *Andrew Muckley*

Right: Drawn blinds on four-wheeler No DW14146 (built Swindon 1902) while the vehicle was in use as a store. *Andrew Muckley*

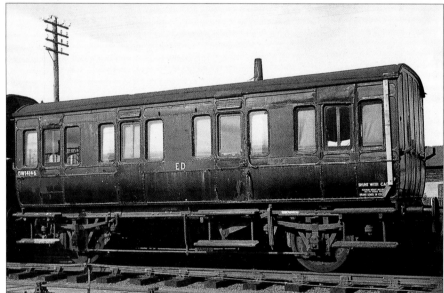

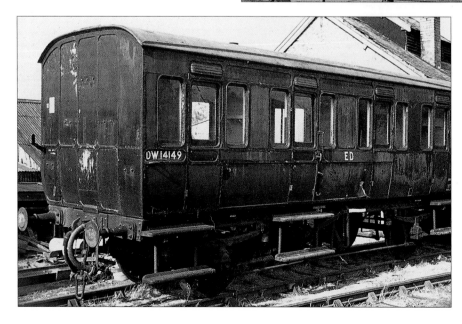

Left: Four-wheeler DW14149 had a 17ft wheelbase — as quoted on the underframe — and was vacuum-braked. Like its companion, it had double foot boards. *Andrew Muckley*

Above: Kerry station pictured in 1904. It is interesting to note that, despite the wide array of enamel signs, not one provides the passenger with the information that this is, in fact, the terminus of the short branch from Abermule. *SLS collection*

Below: Perhaps as a reflection of the lack of signs, passenger services on the Kerry branch ceased on 9 February 1932. This view, recorded long after closure, shows the station building intact, although the fascinating collection of Edwardian posters is now no more. A Dean 0-6-0 stands at the platform with a short freight while the railway staff (in the distance) watch the photographer with interest. Freight services over the 3¾-mile branch, which originally opened in March 1863 (freight) and July 1863 (passenger), would survive until May 1956. *SLS collection*

Above: Among antiquated signals that passed into state ownership on Nationalisation in 1948 was the well-preserved Kerry-branch Distant at Abermule. *Ian Allan Library*

NATIONAL COAL BOARD
SENDER   Date 18 JAN 1960 194
Sneyd Collieries Limited
COBRIDGE, L.M. & Rly. (N.S. Section)
A/c   JAMES EDGE LIMITED

TO
LLANRHAIADR MOCHNANT
G. W. Rly.   C.A.M.   Secn.
Via CREWE & W'CHURCH

                                    T   Cwt.
                        Weight   14   6
Owner and
No. of Wagon 35154
Description   HOUSE COAL GROUP 3
Consignee   J P JONES
                                    O C

Above left: On a hot summer's day in 1959 the author caught a glimpse of the old Cambrian at Blodwell Junction, photographing Ivatt Mogul No 46505 running round a ballast train from Nantmawr Quarries to Oswestry. Note the two short-post signals in background (left). *Author*

Above right: Four years before most of the Tanat Valley line closed, a delivery from the Potteries to keep the home fires burning with Group 3 house coal. *Author's collection*

Below: History achieved. The last working to the quarry at Nantmawr, on 21 October 1971, comprised Class 24 No 5048 and the brake van in which Bob Miller and the author were passengers. *R. W. Miller*

Upper right: A Llanfyllin-branch train from Oswestry, formed by Ivatt Mogul No 46512 and two compartment coaches, calls at Carreghofa Halt, less than a mile from the terminus. The halt dated from 1938 and was GWR property for only a decade. *Andrew Muckley*

Lower right: The Tanat Valley line closed to passengers in January 1951. Trains from Oswestry ran 19½ miles to a low-platform terminus at Llangynog, under the shadow of the Berwyn Mountains. Here 0-4-2 tank No 1412 awaits departure with the 6.55pm to Oswestry on 1 July 1950. The journey, with 10 intermediate stops, took about 1¼ hours. *R. W. Miller collection*

Upper left: Wrexham was linked with the main line at Ellesmere by a branch of almost 13 miles, which ran through an industrial area on the outskirts of Wrexham and became rural on entering Shropshire. An 0-4-2 tank calls at Wrexham Central with the 1.30pm motor train on 24 August 1961. *R. W. Miller collection*

Centre left: On 18 August 1962 — only weeks before withdrawal of the passenger service (at the start of the 1962 winter timetable) — 0-4-2 tank No 1438 takes water at Wrexham Central before departing with the 6.35pm to Ellesmere. *Author's collection*

Below: On 1 October 1955 the single-coach auto-train forming the 2.40pm service from Ellesmere to Wrexham pauses at Marchwiel, the last intermediate station before arrival at Wrexham Central. Motive power on this occasion was provided by '14xx' 0-4-2T No 1432, the trailer being W243W. Passenger services over this route ceased on 10 September 1962, although freight on the northernmost section of the Cambrian, via Wrexham, would survive for a further two decades. *SLS collection*

NARROW-GAUGE LINES

Two light railways closely associated with the Cambrian were detached from British Railways after Nationalisation and subsequently became highly successful lines under new ownership. The Vale of Rheidol (VoR) opened in 1902, and the Welshpool & Llanfair was completed a few months later, both passing to the GWR upon Grouping in 1922/3 and thence to BR's Western Region upon Nationalisation.

After being marketed as the last home of steam on British Rail, the Vale of Rheidol was sold to private owners in March 1989, the British Railways Board stipulating that the successful bidder run a seasonal passenger service for at least five years. In its final years of ownership, BR successfully developed summer passenger services, doubling to 52,000 the number of passengers carried in the 1960s. Tourist leaflets stated that 'Nowhere in Britain is there scenery more beautiful than that of the Rheidol Valley'. The year 1967 saw the locomotives and coaches repainted in BR blue and given its new double-arrow logo. In 1968 VoR trains were diverted from their original station at Aberystwyth into the much more tourist-convenient Carmarthen Bay platform of the main station, and cheap morning-only return fares were introduced. A BR initiative in 1970 was the formation of a VoR Supporters Association, to publicise the line and to work towards a future under BR ownership, management and operation. By 1972 membership had reached nearly 600.

In contrast to the VoR (which was sold for a second time in 1996 and is run by professional staff), the Welshpool & Llanfair Light Railway is volunteer-orientated, having been run since 1963 by a Guarantee Company of enthusiasts led by a Board of Directors. The earlier closure of this most charming of rural lines extended over a quarter of a century: the GWR withdrew passenger services in February 1931, but it was not until Bonfire Night 1956 that it was closed by BR. When closure was being considered, local authorities complained to the TUCC that they had been unable to object because of not being notified, but they finally agreed after further talks. Within a few days of closure a preservation society had been formed and, after reconstitution for legal reasons, operated part of the line from the Llanfair end, following which members began an extension of nearly three miles from Sylfaen to a new station on the outskirts of Welshpool, thereby achieving their ambition of reopening almost the entire line of 1903 to passengers.

Upper left: A Vale of Rheidol Supporters' Association was launched by Stoke Division in 1970. Among enticements were an enamelled badge, a souvenir brochure and reasonable access by arrangement to visit the locomotive stabling point at Aberystwyth. *Author's collection*

Lower left: A London Midland Region leaflet from 1966 extolling the virtues of the Vale of Rheidol, then BR's only narrow-gauge line. The season started with a special three-day Easter opening, when trains were advertised as departing from its platform still adjacent to (rather than part of) Aberystwyth's main station. *Author's collection*

Above: Summer on the Vale of Rheidol. No 7 *Owain Glyndwr*, in blue livery, makes a spirited start from Aberystwyth past the former standard-gauge engine shed (now housing narrow-gauge engines) on 3 August 1972. *R. W. Miller*

THE WELSHPOOL & LLANFAIR LIGHT RAILWAY PRESERVATION CO. LTD.

THE WELSHPOOL EXTENSION PROJECT

This leaflet is an introduction to the most exciting project that the Welshpool & Llanfair Railway has so far undertaken—the re-opening of the final 2¾ miles of the line from its present terminus at Sylfaen to Welshpool. The railway has been operated for the last sixteen years by a 'guarantee' company—controlled by its enthusiast members through a Board of Directors. When it was formed in 1960, it had as its principal aim the operation of train services over the entire length of the line, and this ambition has formed the basis of all policy decisions since that time.

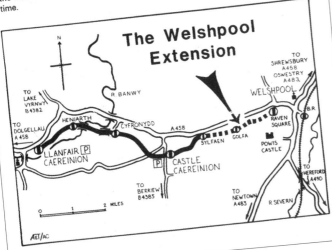

Above: Watched by summer picknickers, No 822 *The Earl* attacks the steep bank from Welshpool to Golfa in May 2002. *R. W. Miller*

Left: The enthusiasts who took over the Welshpool & Llanfair Light Railway lost little time in starting to turn their dream of an extension to Welshpool into reality. A fund-raising leaflet explained that the company 'is not just a supporters' club. It actually owns and operates the railway!' *Author's collection*

Upper right: 'The decidedly foreign atmosphere' of trains on the Welshpool & Llanfair Light Railway (as described in *Railways Restored*) is reflected by an arrival at Llanfair Caereinion station on 5 May 2002. The locomotive is No 823 *The Countess. R. W. Miller*

Lower right: The Ffestiniog Railway's *Palmerston* was hired to the Cambrian for use on the Vale of Rheidol in 1913/14, an arrangement only terminated by the outbreak of war. Once hostilities were over traffic grew, and *Palmerston* was again hired in 1921/2. The locomotive has now been rebuilt and restored for use on the Ffestiniog and is seen here at Tan-y-Bwlch on 23 October 1994. *Melvyn Hopwood*

5. LOCOMOTIVES AND SHEDS

By the end of the first year of Nationalisation there were only 14 ex-Cambrian Railways locomotives still in stock, but as their number dwindled enthusiasts held them in ever-increasing affection. Eleven were 0-6-0s of Jones's '89' class, the rest narrow-gauge tanks. The 0-6-0s had been scrapped by 1954, soon after a start had been made on updating the locomotives working on the Cambrian lines, which had begun when replacement of the Jones and ex-GWR 'Dean Goods' 0-6-0s still working on the Mid-Wales line became urgent. As Collett 0-6-0s were too heavy, ex-LMS Ivatt '464xx' Moguls took over.

As well as being attracted by the Dean 0-6-0s, enthusiasts travelled to Mid-Wales to see 'Dukedog' 4-4-0s, of which there were generally about 20 on the system from 1939 to 1957, the last, No 9017 departing for preservation in the autumn of 1960. (The 'Dukedogs' are vividly recalled in the IA SBS video of the BBC *Railway Roundabout* programme, in which two are featured hauling a Talyllyn Railway special from Shrewsbury in 1960, shortly before they were withdrawn. The video of the 1962 programme features No 7803 *Barcote Manor* hauling the 'Cambrian Coast Express' from Shrewsbury.)

Elsewhere, Swindon-built '75xxx' 4-6-0s progressively replaced 'Manors' of almost identical size which had worked on the Cambrian for some years, during which time they had grown in number from five in the 1940s to 14 in 1960. Their ranks had been depleted to four by 1963 (although a further five remained shedded at Shrewsbury), and all had gone by 1966. Two years earlier your author 'footplated' home from Aberystwyth to Welshpool on No 7800 *Torquay Manor*, hauling the mid-day express to Shrewsbury. With a gale blowing in from Cardigan Bay on a bitterly cold winter's day the ride was exhilarating, especially while pounding Talerddig — though not for the driver and fireman.

As steam was gradually replaced by DMUs and (chiefly on freight duties) diesel locomotives, steam sheds and sub-sheds of varying sizes closed progressively. The last to go went in 1965/6, when Oswestry, Penmaenpool, Portmadoc and Pwllheli ceased operation and Machynlleth was converted to diesel. Steam's funeral took place on 4 March 1967, when two '75xxx' 4-6-0s hauled the last up and down workings of the 'Cambrian Coast Express'.

Upper right: Whatever their condition, the 'Manors' always looked powerful, especially when calling at rural stations like Carno, where the fireman of an up stopping train is seen exchanging a token. In many ways the photograph epitomises much that was interesting and attractive on the Cambrian. *Andrew Muckley*

Lower right: With a quiet head of steam No 7800 *Torquay Manor* awaits departure from a deserted platform at Welshpool for a non-stop run to Shrewsbury on 29 January 1964. *Author's collection*

Below: 'Manor' 4-6-0s were first allocated to the Cambrian in 1943, when they became the first locomotives able to pull expresses over Talerddig unaided. They could haul nine corridor coaches — three more than the 'Dukedog' 4-4-0s. No 7808 *Cookham Manor* looks rather run-down at Machynlleth shed in August 1964. *Andrew Muckley*

Left: Through the years 'Manors' worked a number of specials, including that for the Talyllyn Railway members in September 1965, double-headed by Nos 7812 *Erlestoke Manor* and 7802 *Bradley Manor*, to which the headboard is being affixed before departure from Shrewsbury. *R. W. Miller*

Right: Preserved No 7819 *Hinton Manor* was one of two Severn Valley Railway locomotives which worked the 'Cardigan Bay Express' when steam returned to the Cambrian in 1987. *British Railways*

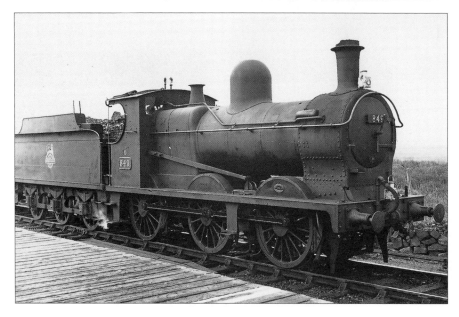

Left: A veteran Cambrian 0-6-0 still working in 1953 was ex-GWR No 849. The setting is Dovey Junction. *Ian Allan Library*

Lower right: Ex-Cambrian 0-6-0 No 855 being coaled at Oswestry in May 1953. *Ian Allan Library*

Above: Working on the Cambrian for longer than the 'Manors' were ex-GWR Dean 0-6-0s, which before World War 2 constituted the most numerous class, totalling 47 by 1938. No 2538 passes Abermule with a heavy main-line goods in the 1950s, by which time their numbers were being thinned. The last of the Deans was withdrawn in 1957. *R. W. Miller collection*

Upper right: Ivatt 2-6-0s were introduced after World War 2, and a number were found on different parts of the Cambrian. No 46524 departs Barmouth with an early-afternoon working to Dovey Junction in May 1963. *R. F. Roberts*

Above: Ex-GWR 0-6-0s of the '2251' class worked on the main line from the late 1930s, and 16 were on the system between 1946 and 1959. Occasionally they worked the 'Cambrian Coast Express'. No 2200 is seen at Aberystwyth shed in spring 1953. *Ian Allan Library*

Below: Ex-GWR Moguls were among visitors to the system which they often reached by working through the Dee Valley between Ruabon and Morfa Mawddach. No 7339 of the '43xx' class, at Barmouth in the autumn of 1961. *R. F. Roberts*

Lower right: Standard 4-6-0 No 75047 being turned by one man at Machynlleth. The locomotive just fits on the turntable. Sister engine No 75024 was the last to be re-tubed at Oswestry Works before closure in 1966. *Andrew Muckley*

Upper left: Oswestry Locomotive Works was open for just a century from 1866, while the Carriage & Wagon Works had a slightly shorter life, closing in the summer of 1964. Afterwards the buildings were sold and used for a variety of purposes, and part of the site became a shopping centre. In May 1953 No 78005 passes with an afternoon working from Whitchurch to Welshpool. *R. W. Miller*

Centre left: In June 1954 two veteran Cambrian 0-6-0s were employed at Oswestry Works to supply boiler heat while the main system was under repair; these were ex-GWR Nos 855 (nearer the camera) and 844. *R. W. Miller*

Lower left: No 844, which had its whistles fixed on the firebox, was scrapped in August 1954, by which time it was 36 years old. No 855 followed in October, at the age of 30. *R. W. Miller*

Upper right: The Cambrian's largest shed was in the fork of the Whitchurch and Gobowen lines just north of Oswestry station. Though small compared with Crewe locomotive sheds about 30 miles away, it attracted enthusiasts because of its varied allocation. On 29 July 1951 locomotives on shed included 'Manor' 4-6-0 No 7823 *Hook Norton Manor*, 'Dukedog' 4-4-0 No 9026, '16xx' 0-6-0PT No 1604 and '2251' 0-6-0s Nos 2244 and 3208. *SLS/W. Potter*

Centre right: Oswestry new shed on 29 March 1953, with 0-4-2 tank No 1459 in foreground. *Ian Allan Library*

Lower right: Cambrian Railway Society depot at Oswestry: No 7822 *Foxcote Manor* being flagged over the public level crossing outside the company depot on 16 June 2002. The imposing main station building stands behind. *R. W. Miller*

Left: 'Dukedog' 4-4-0 No 9018 stands outside the shed at Machynlleth on 23 June 1958. By this date these once familiar locomotives were approaching the twilight of their career, and only six remained in service. Built in April 1938, No 9018 was intended to carry the name *Earl of Birkenhead*, but the naming never took place. The locomotive would be withdrawn in June 1960. *R. E. Vincent*

Above: Aberystwyth shed on 18 June 1963, with No 7810 *Drayton Manor* and Standard 2-6-4 tank No 80096 carrying an 89C (Machynlleth) shedplate.
R. W. Miller collection

Right: An unidentified 'Manor' and 4-4-0 No 9022 at Aberystwyth shed in May 1953.
Ian Allan Library

Top: The two-road shed at Penmaenpool was one of the smallest built by the Cambrian Railways, which opened it in 1869. At Nationalisation its sole allocation was an 0-4-2 tank. The shed was in use until the Morfa Mawddach–Dolgellau section of the Dee Valley route closed in January 1965. *A. C. Gilbert*

Centre: Portmadoc. In 1949 this was home to seven 0-6-0s, including some 'Dean Goods', and two '45xx' 2-6-2 tanks. The station is in the distance. *Ian Allan Library*

Left: Moat Lane shed, close to the junction, became semi-derelict structurally soon after Nationalisation and was partially demolished. In the summer of 1955 the by now roofless two-road shed was home to locomotives ancient and modern — 'Dean Goods' 0-6-0 No 2516 and Ivatt Mogul No 46522. *R. W. Miller*

CHRONOLOGY

Above: Brecon shed, closed in 1962, was a Brecon & Merthyr Railway structure; a Cambrian shed had been demolished by the GWR in the 1930s. 'Dean Goods' No 2541 is seen stabled beside an unidentified 0-6-0 in May 1952. *Author's collection*

The following is a selective chronology of line closures since Nationalisation.

	Passengers	Goods
Feeder routes		
Afon Wen–Caernarvon	7 Dec 1964	7 Dec 1964
Caernarvon–Menai Bridge	5 Jan 1970	5 Feb 1972
Aberystwyth–Strata Florida	14 Dec 1964	2 Dec 1963
Strata Florida–Carmarthen	22 Feb 1965	16 Mar 1964
Llangollen–Bala Junction	13 Dec 1964	13 Dec 1964
Bala Junction–Dolgellau	18 Jan 1965	18 Jan 1965
Ruabon–Llangollen	18 Jan 1965	1 Apr 1968
Oswestry–Gobowen	7 Nov 1966	6 Dec 1971
Former Cambrian Railways lines		
Cemmes Road–Dinas Mawddwy	1 Jan 1931	6 Sep 1950
Llanrhaiadr Mochnant–Llangynog	15 Jan 1951	1 Jul 1952
Abermule–Kerry	9 Feb 1931	1 May 1956
Welshpool–Llanfair Caereinion	9 Feb 1931	5 Nov 1956
Blodwell Junction–Llanrhaiadr Mochnant	15 Jan 1951	5 Dec 1960
Llynclys Junction–Blodwell Junction	15 Jan 1951	(mothballed)
Wrexham–Pickhill	10 Sep 1962	4 May 1981
Pickhill–Ellesmere	10 Sep 1962	27 Mar 1965
Llanidloes–Talyllyn	31 Dec 1962	31 Dec 1962
Aberdovey Harbour branch	14 Aug 1867	4 May 1964
Whitchurch–Oswestry	18 Jan 1965	29 Mar 1965
Whitchurch–Oswestry–Buttington	18 Jan 1965	18 Jan 1965
Gobowen–Oswestry–Blodwell	7 Nov 1966	(mothballed)
Llanymynech–Llanfyllin	18 Jan 1965	2 Nov 1964
Barmouth Junction–Dolgellau	18 Jan 1965	14 Dec 1964

Front cover: 'Manor' No 7822 *Foxcote Manor* runs into Talerddig with a down train to the coast in August 1964, the last year that 'Manors' dominated passenger services on the Cambrian. *J. B. Snell/Colour-Rail*

Back cover, top: 'Dukedog' No 9015 is pictured soon after leaving Llandre on a stopping service from Aberystwyth to Machynlleth on 2 August 1958. *T. B. Owen*

Back cover, centre: On the same day, '43xx' 2-6-0 No 6335 finds itself on a glamorous duty heading the 'Cambrian Coast Express' with a smart rake of chocolate and cream Mk1s on the last leg of its journey into Aberystwyth. *T. B. Owen*

Back cover, bottom: Three years later, BR Standard Class 2 2-6-0 No 78000 has moved into the area and is seen at Llanbadarn Crossing soon after starting its journey from Aberystwyth to Shrewsbury on 6 August 1961. *T. B. Owen*